D is for Drinking Gourd

An African American Alphabet

Written by Nancy I. Sanders and Illustrated by E. B. Lewis

SCHOLASTIC INC.
New York Toronto London Auckland Sydney
Mexico City New Delhi Hong Kong Buenos Aires

ISBN-13: 978-0-545-13053-0
ISBN-10: 0-545-13053-0

Text copyright © 2007 by Nancy I. Sanders. Illustrations copyright © 2007 by E. B. Lewis.
All rights reserved. Published by Scholastic Inc., 557 Broadway, New York, NY 10012, by arrangement with Sleeping Bear Press. SCHOLASTIC and associated logos are trademarks and/or registered trademarks of Scholastic Inc.

12 11 10 9 8 7 6 5 4 3 2   9 10 11 12 13/0

Printed in the U.S.A.   08

First Scholastic printing, October 2008

God bless our native land,
Land of the newly free,
Oh may she ever stand
For truth and liberty.

from *God Bless Our Native Land*
by Frances E. W. Harper

"Let our people go!" they cried
in speeches or with pen in hand.
A is for abolitionists
who were willing to take a stand.

In the years before the Civil War, abolitionists were a group of people who tried to bring slavery to an end. Men and women traveled throughout the states speaking against the evils of slavery. A strong woman of faith and a former slave, Sojourner Truth was a powerful speaker in support of abolition and women's rights. Frederick Douglass escaped from bondage to become one of the most important abolitionist leaders. His autobiography caused many others to understand what slavery was really like. Journalist, doctor, explorer, and leading abolitionist who frequently spoke with Douglass, Martin Delany was appointed as a major in the Union Army during the Civil War.

The black press, newspapers owned and operated by African Americans, printed numerous articles challenging fellow Americans to join together in the fight against slavery. The most famous newspaper of all, *The North Star*, was co-edited by Frederick Douglass and Martin Delany.

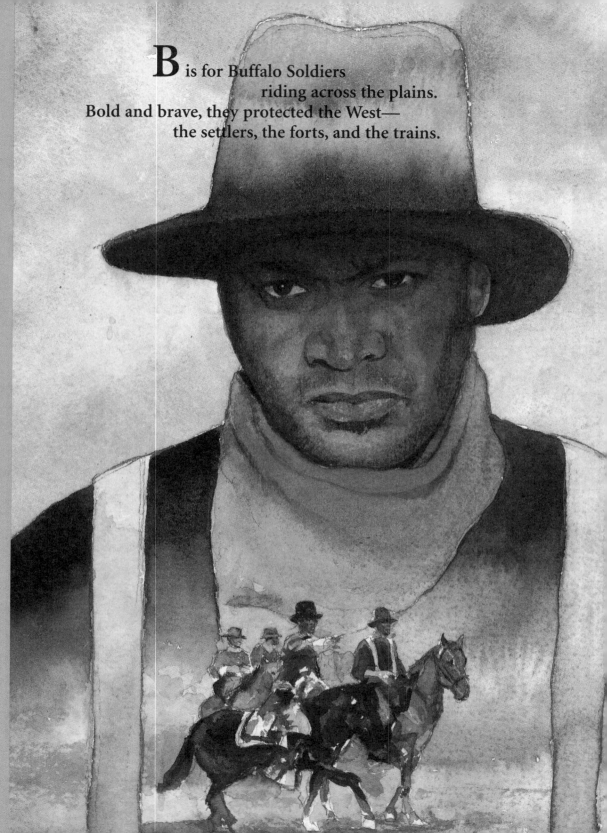

After the Civil War, African American soldiers were stationed on the western frontier. The Native Americans gave them the honorable nickname of "Buffalo Soldiers."

When the U.S. government treated Native Americans unfairly in attempting to take over and settle their land, various tribes responded by attacking wagon trains, settlers, stagecoaches, and trains. Both the Infantry and Cavalry units of Buffalo Soldiers were called out to offer protection from these attacks. More than a dozen men were awarded the Congressional Medal of Honor.

To test bicycles for military use, in 1897 the 25th Infantry rode bicycles from Montana to St. Louis, Missouri. As these Buffalo Soldiers traveled through the countryside, onlookers gathered to cheer them on.

B is for Buffalo Soldiers
riding across the plains.
Bold and brave, they protected the West—
the settlers, the forts, and the trains.

Bb

C c

Sweat-stained hats and spurs that jingled,
rodeos with daredevil clowns,
C is for the cowboys
and cattle drives to railroad towns.

During the late 1800s, more than 5,000 black cowboys rode the Chisholm Trail, driving cattle from Texas north to the railroad in Abilene, Kansas.

Rodeo stars such as Nat Love and Bill Pickett drew huge crowds. Love was well known for his keen sharpshooting abilities. Pickett was famous for his technique known as bulldogging where he bit a steer on the muzzle and wrestled it to the ground. Pickett was the first African American admitted to the National Rodeo Cowboy Hall of Fame.

Marshall Bass Reeves kept law and order throughout the West. Wearing disguises and speaking several Native American languages, he brought over 3,000 outlaws to justice during the 32 years he served as Deputy U.S. Marshal in the Indian Territory.

Numerous African Americans settled in the wild, Wild West. Encouraged by Benjamin "Pap" Singleton, thousands of families left the South in 1879. Many established all-black towns in Kansas. These pioneers, cowboys, and settlers were known as Exodusters.

The Big Dipper was commonly called the Drinking Gourd because it reminded people of the dry gourds they used to dip water out of a bucket for a drink. At night, fugitive slaves looked up at the Drinking Gourd to locate the North Star. The North Star helped guide them to the northern states where they would be free.

Men and women known as "conductors" often hid runaways in their homes along a secret route called the Underground Railroad. People such as William Still, David Ruggles, and William Whipper used their own money to help hundreds escape north. Harriet Tubman, or Moses as some called her, journeyed deep into the southern states. She personally led over 300 slaves to freedom.

Spirituals and songs such as "Follow the Drinking Gourd" often contained secret codes to pass important information from one person to the next about escaping on the Underground Railroad.

D is for Drinking Gourd,
and the North Star that led through the night
from station to station on the Underground Railroad,
escaping on a dangerous flight.

E e

E is for Emancipation,
a big word that means to be free.
When people heard the proclamation,
it was a day of jubilee!

On January 1, 1863, President Lincoln issued the Emancipation Proclamation. This important document officially freed all the slaves in the southern states. Many referred to this as the day of jubilee because great rejoicing took place.

The news did not reach Texas until more than two years later. On June 19, 1865, General Granger rode into Galveston, Texas and read the Emancipation Proclamation aloud for all to hear. A great celebration was held.

Juneteenth is a special holiday held each year in June to remember the historic day emancipation was brought to Texas. Friends and families gather to celebrate with festivals and parades all across America.

There were more than 5,000 black patriots fighting for independence in the American Revolution. African Americans fought in every major battle of the war.

Crispus Attucks, the first person to die in the fight for liberty, was killed during the Boston Massacre. Prince Estabrook and Peter Salem were minutemen at Lexington and Concord when the first shots were fired.

The early American government did not allow men of color to participate as political leaders, so there were no signatures of African Americans on the Declaration of Independence. Richard Allen, Absalom Jones, and James Forten, however, met just down the street from Independence Hall in Philadelphia, the new nation's capital. These Founding Fathers organized free blacks, and founded numerous societies and churches. Their tireless efforts helped bring an end to the slave trade and eventually slavery itself.

Just before the U.S. Constitution was written, Richard Allen and Absalom Jones organized the Free African Society to help the poor, promote justice, and provide a place to worship. Because it was the first organization of its kind for African Americans, this society was a monumental step in the history of America.

Ff

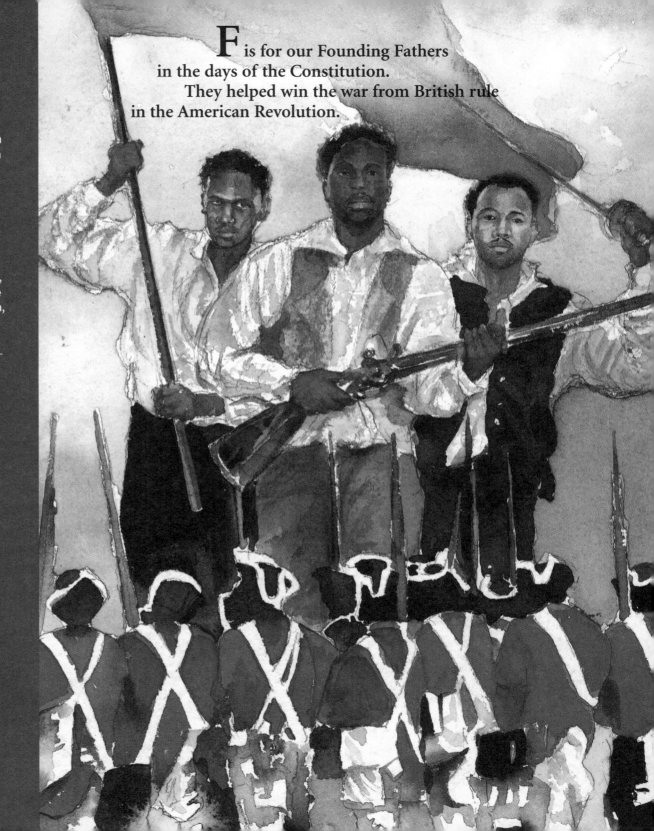

F is for our Founding Fathers
in the days of the Constitution.
They helped win the war from British rule
in the American Revolution.

Thousands moved from the South to the North.
That's why **G** is for Great Migration.
Families went to the cities looking for jobs
and a better education.

When World War I began, America's doors closed to the arrival of European immigrants. At the same time, northern industries needed more workers to produce manufactured goods for the war. Industries advertised throughout the South, inviting African Americans to move to northern cities such as Pittsburgh and Chicago.

Because of the increase of violence against African Americans, the South had become a very dangerous place to stay. Also, segregation laws in southern states made life unbearable, taking away voting privileges, educational opportunities, and equal rights. Entire black communities packed their bags and moved north.

Many societies, such as the National Urban League, were formed to help family members find a place to stay, get a job, and adjust to their new surroundings.

Nannie Helen Burroughs believed that education was the key to a successful future. She established the National Training School for Women and Girls in Washington, D.C., and was an influential leader in many societies and clubs.

H h

Poetry, paintings, photography... the stage!
Hit songs at the top of the chart;
H is for Harlem Renaissance,
a great birth of culture and art.

People flocked to Harlem in the 1920s. Artists, writers, musicians, and political activists gathered in this New York neighborhood to express their ideas.

Langston Hughes, one of the most famous writers of all time, is known as the poet laureate of Harlem.

Among her other writings, Zora Neale Hurston wrote down collections of folk tales that reveal what life was like living in the South.

An outstanding student, athlete, singer, and activist for civil rights, Paul Robeson chose a career in acting. His starring role in the stage performance of *Othello* won him great fame.

Known as the Empress of the Blues, Bessie Smith captivated audiences with her rich voice and unique style of singing.

Augusta Savage was a famous sculptor whose work included lifelike portraits of African American heroes.

As a photographer, James VanDerZee captured the Harlem Renaissance on film.

There have been many inventions made by African Americans. Norbert Rillieux invented a better process for making sugar. Elijah McCoy invented a machine to oil engines on trains and ships. Jan Ernst Matzeliger invented a machine that made it easier to manufacture shoes. Lewis Latimer invented a better filament to be used in lightbulbs. A self-made millionaire, Madam C. J. Walker invented hair products and beauty creams.

Modern inventions include the Super Soaker, a popular squirt gun invented by Lonnie Johnson. Kenneth Dunkley invented the Three-Dimensional Viewing Glasses, which make it possible for readers to view an ordinary magazine in stunning 3-D. Scientists and engineers are constantly working on new inventions such as Thomas Mensah's fiber optics research, James McLurkin's micro-robots design, and Patricia Bath's invention of a tool that uses a laser to treat blindness.

Ii

I is for Inventions,
new gadgets for people to use.
Inventors have ideas for all sorts of items
from hair products to machines that make shoes.

J j

Trumpets playing to a syncopated beat,
crowds forming just to hear,
J is for Jazz and jazz musician.
There's a new song in the air!

Louis Armstrong was known by his many fans as "Satchmo." A genius with his trumpet, Armstrong was also world famous for his rich, deep voice. He was the most important soloist in the history of jazz.

Duke Ellington and his band brought jazz into the hearts and homes of America. Through radio shows, live performances, and recordings, millions listened to the songs Ellington wrote, played, and directed.

One of the greatest voices in jazz, Ella Fitzgerald won many honors and awards.

Sarah Vaughan's amazing vocal range and singing ability won her the nickname, "Divine One."

Born in New Orleans, Wynton Marsalis uses his trumpet to bring jazz to audiences today. Through television and workshops, Marsalis also teaches about the history of jazz. He is co-founder and artistic director of a program in New York City called Jazz at Lincoln Center.

Lighting candles, telling stories,
reciting an inspirational quote;
K is for Kwanzaa,
a celebration of unity and hope.

Family and friends gather to celebrate Kwanzaa, a holiday that lasts from December 26 through January 1.

Developed by Maulana Karenga in 1966, the word Kwanzaa means "first fruits" in Swahili.

The seven principles of Kwanzaa are unity, self-determination, collective work and responsibility, cooperative economics, purpose, creativity, and faith.

The seven symbols of Kwanzaa are fruits, vegetables, and nuts; a placemat; a candle-holder; ears of corn; gifts; the cup of unity; and seven candles.

Kwanzaa is a time to celebrate important achievements by African Americans. There have been numerous accomplishments throughout the years, especially in the world of science and medicine. Scientist George Washington Carver invented an amazing variety of products from crops such as sweet potatoes and peanuts. Biologist Ernest E. Just discovered important information about how cells work. Dr. Charles Drew conducted extensive research on blood, making success-ful blood banks possible in hospitals today. Dr. Jane Wright and her father, Dr. Louis Wright, were pioneers in cancer research.

L is for Little Rock Nine,
the students who integrated school
at Little Rock, Arkansas's, Central High—
protected under military rule.

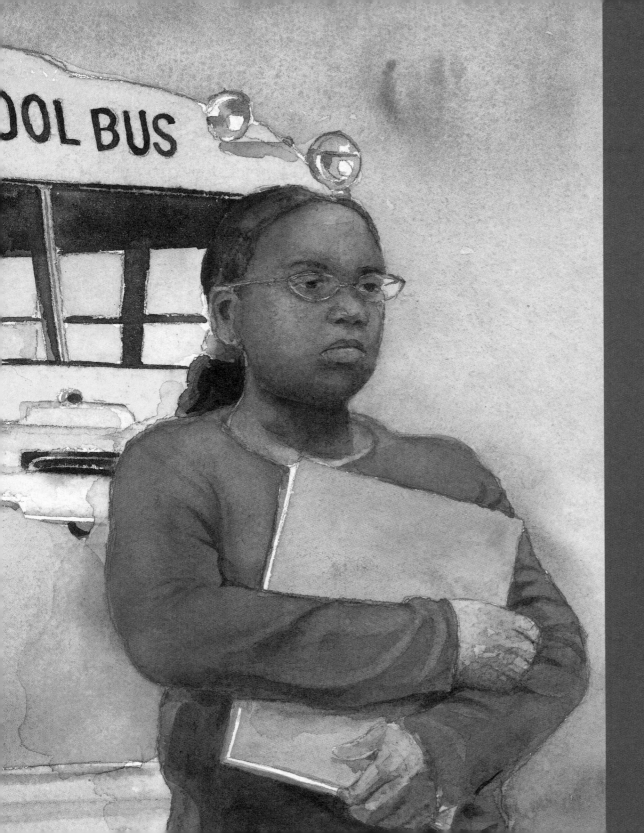

Before the 1960s, many schools in the southern states were segregated. This meant that black children could not attend the same schools as white children.

In 1957 the Little Rock school board offered permission for families to integrate their children into the local high school. Dorothy Bates, leader of the National Association for the Advancement of Colored People (NAACP), volunteered to help. Against great opposition and many threats of violence, nine high school students bravely tried to attend the all-white Central High School in Little Rock, Arkansas. When the governor of Arkansas refused to allow them to enroll, President Dwight D. Eisenhower ordered federal troops to step in. The heroic young women and men were able to attend school with soldiers by their side, offering military protection and support.

The nine courageous students who integrated Central High School were Minni-Jean Brown, Elizabeth Eckford, Ernest Green, Thelma Mothershed, Melba Patillo, Gloria Ray, Terrance Roberts, Jefferson Thomas, and Carlotta Walls.

Ll

M m

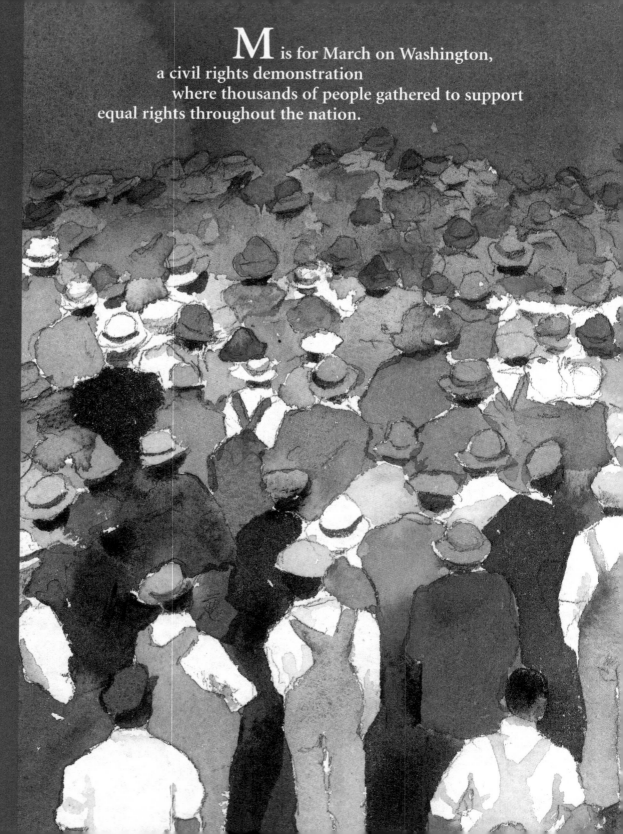

M is for March on Washington,
a civil rights demonstration
where thousands of people gathered to support
equal rights throughout the nation.

On August 28, 1963, nearly 250,000 people gathered in Washington, D.C. to support civil rights and the end of segregation. This demonstration helped influence Congress to pass President John F. Kennedy's Civil Rights Act. People from all across the U.S. gathered at the Washington Monument and marched peacefully to the Lincoln Memorial where prayers, songs, and speeches were heard.

The most famous speech that day was "I Have a Dream" by Dr. Martin Luther King Jr. A strong supporter of nonviolent action, Dr. King was president of the Southern Christian Leadership Conference (SCLC). Pastor of the Dexter Avenue Baptist Church in Montgomery, Alabama, Dr. King led numerous marches and crusades in support of equal rights, including the famous children's march and the Montgomery Bus Boycott, sparked when Rosa Parks was arrested because she refused to move to the back of the bus. Dr. King was awarded the Nobel Peace Prize in 1964. In 1968 people all around the world mourned when they heard the shocking news that he had been assassinated.

N is for NAACP
and the legal help it provides.
This important organization
has saved countless numbers of lives.

N
n

Formed in 1909, the National Association for the Advancement of Colored People (NAACP) has been a powerful voice in legal victories, educational opportunities, economic improvement, and civil rights. Its lawyers have worked hard in successful court battles to protect people from injustices such as mob violence, false accusations, and racial discrimination.

W. E. B. Du Bois was among the founding members of the NAACP. An outstanding scholar, important historian, and monumental leader, he dedicated most of his life to the pursuit of equal rights in America.

The Crisis was the official journal of the NAACP. As its editor, Du Bois featured news updates and published a variety of works by Harlem Renaissance writers.

Thurgood Marshall was a lawyer for the NAACP who won many landmark court cases. In 1967 he became the first African American justice of the Supreme Court of the United States.

Outstanding athletes each do their best,
inspiring both young and old.
O is for Olympic medals—
the bronze, the silver, the gold.

Athletes set amazing Olympic records in track and field. In 1936 Jesse Owens was the star of the Berlin Olympics. He raced to victory after victory, winning four gold medals. Nearly 50 years later, Carl Lewis followed in Owens' footsteps to win four gold medals in the 1984 Olympics. Competing over several Olympics, Jackie Joyner-Kersee won bronze, silver, and gold medals for a total of six in all.

Muhammad Ali was one of many boxers who won the gold medal.

Gymnast Dominique Dawes and ice skater Debra Thomas each won medals for outstanding performance and skill.

Champions such as Bill Russell, Cheryl Miller, Earvin "Magic" Johnson, and Michael Jordan joined their Olympic teams for thrilling performances on the basketball court.

In 2002 a new star was born! Vonetta Flowers sped down snowy slopes to a surprising victory in a bright red bobsled with her racing partner, Jill Bakken. Flowers became the first African American to win a gold medal in the Winter Olympics.

Pp

Government leaders make important decisions for people in their cities and states. P is for Politics and politicians and political candidates.

Many African American men and women have been elected as mayors, governors, senators, and other political officials.

Hiram Revels and Blanche Bruce became the first African Americans to serve in the United States Senate. They were elected during Reconstruction, a short period of time after the Civil War when hundreds of African Americans were elected to government positions throughout the South.

One of the most influential members of President Franklin Roosevelt's Black Cabinet was Mary McLeod Bethune, who was also the advisor of several other presidents. The Black Cabinet gave advice to the president about how to help African Americans get better housing, food, and jobs.

His popularity and enthusiasm brought Barack Obama to center stage in the political arena with his 2004 election to the United States Senate. He is the fifth African American to serve in the Senate, following in the footsteps of such political leaders as Hiram Revels, Blanche Bruce, Edward Brooke, and Carol Moseley Braun.

Colin Powell and Condaleeza Rice became two of the most important government officials in America. During the years George W. Bush was president, each was appointed secretary of state.

Quilting has been a tradition passed down through many generations. Patterns have interesting names such as the Ohio Star, Wagon Wheel, Crossroads, and Log Cabin. Before the Civil War, quilts may have been used to help slaves escaping north along the Underground Railroad. A quilt hung on a porch rail might be a signal that the house was a safe place to stop for help.

Quilt artist Harriet Powers was famous for the two Bible quilts she stitched together in the late 1800s. These quilts show pictures of different Bible stories and are on display in museums today.

The tradition of quilting is carried on by Faith Ringgold, a modern-day storytelling artist. Ringgold combines her love of painting, soft sculpture, and quilting to create beautiful quilts that each have a story to tell.

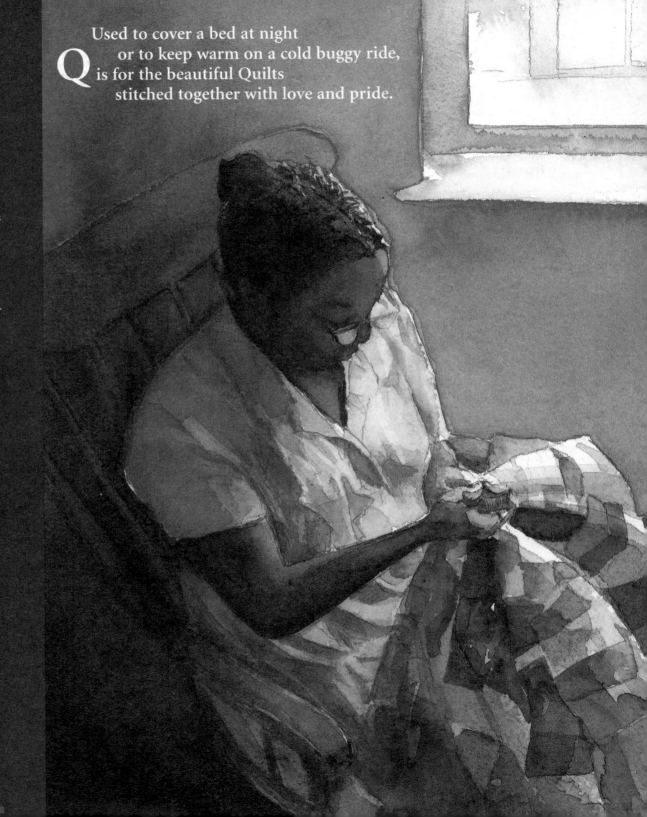

Used to cover a bed at night
  or to keep warm on a cold buggy ride,
Q is for the beautiful Quilts
  stitched together with love and pride.

Black pharaohs in Egypt, ancient empires of gold,
royal caravans to Timbuktu;

R is for African Roots
and the glories that Africa once knew.

Africa has experienced a glorious history, rich with achievement and progress. Long ago, kings with golden scepters lived in royal cities. Skilled crafters produced metalwork, leather, and woven cloth. Farmers grew an abundant variety of crops. Family life was important.

In the eighth century B.C.E., Ethiopia conquered Egypt. For the next hundred years, Ethiopian pharaohs, such as Piankhy and Taharka, ruled along the Nile.

From the 1100s to the 1400s, kingdoms in Africa grew very wealthy and strong. Traders from the north led huge caravans of camels across the Sahara Desert to reach the kingdoms of Ghana, Mali, and Songhay, which were rich in gold.

Timbuktu was a center of learning and faith during the Middle Ages. Scholars from far and wide came to this important city in the heart of Africa to study science, medicine, and literature.

After Columbus sailed to the New World in 1492, European countries established colonies in North and South America. The colony of Jamestown, Virginia was settled in 1607. In 1619 a ship brought 20 Africans to Jamestown. A year later in 1620, the Pilgrims landed at Plymouth Rock, Massachusetts. When Africans first arrived at Jamestown, the colony was still having a hard time surviving in the harsh wilderness. Coming from the kingdom of Ndongo in Angola, Africa, these men and women knew how to grow corn and tobacco, two crops essential to the success of the colony. Many were also blacksmiths, a highly valued skill in colonial days. The earliest African colonists were treated more like indentured servants than slaves. They were able to earn their freedom, own land, vote, and hold office.

Businesses in Europe began to organize the Atlantic Slave Trade. Slave ships sailed back and forth across the Atlantic Ocean. They took captive Africans to America to work as slaves on southern plantations or in cities up north. These ships carried crops or raw goods from the plantations back to Europe. During the Middle Passage, ships sailed from Africa to America carrying hundreds of captives chained below deck. Many Africans suffered and died from the terrible conditions on board slave ships.

The most famous slave rebellion in America was led by Nat Turner in 1831. In 1839 Joseph Cinque led a successful mutiny on board the slave ship, *Amistad*. Enslaved Africans and African Americans revolted many times over the years in their struggle to be free.

Ss

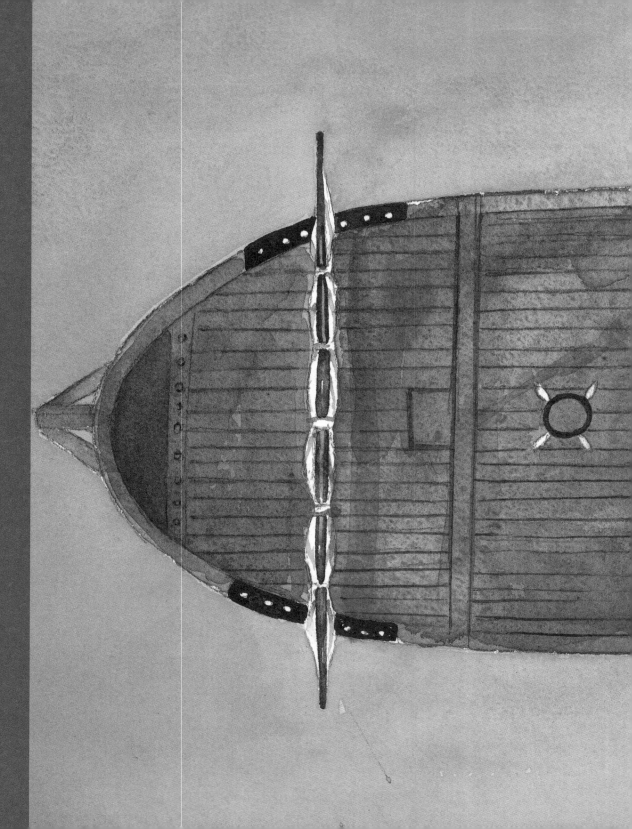

Hard work, little food, hearts heavy with sorrow;
sold away from family and friends;
S is for Slavery, a sad part of our past.
The Civil War finally brought it to an end.

T is for Tuskegee Airmen,
flying their planes through the clouds.
These pilots were heroes in World War II
and won many distinguished awards.

The Tuskegee Airmen were pilots during World War II. They gained international fame for escorting American bombers over enemy territory. Because of their amazing flying abilities, none of the planes they escorted were ever shot down by enemy fighters. One of their top squadron commanders, Benjamin O. Davis Jr. went on to become the first African American general in the Air Force.

Other military heroes included the first African American officers in the U.S. Navy who became known as the Golden Thirteen. These 13 men were chosen to receive officer training in 1944 because of their scholarly achievements, athletic ability, and leadership potential. Their hard work and dedication opened the door for integration at all levels of service in the Navy.

Benjamin Oliver Davis Sr. and his son Benjamin Oliver Davis Jr. both became high-ranking generals in the armed forces.

Women such as Brigadier Generals Clara Adams-Ender and Marcelite Harris accomplished many firsts in their outstanding military careers.

In March, 2007, 200 Tuskegee Airmen received the Congressional Gold Medal.

After the Civil War, the Freedman's Bureau established numerous colleges and universities to help provide education for the newly freed slaves.

Historically black universities such as Howard University, Fisk University, and Tuskegee Institute have provided a higher education for numerous young men and women who went on to become significant achievers and outstanding leaders all across the nation. Many influential leaders during the Civil Rights Movement graduated from historically black universities.

Bishop Daniel Payne of the A.M.E. Church was the first African American president of a college with his appointment at Wilberforce University.

Johnnetta Cole, award-winning educator, became the first woman president of Spelman College.

After graduating from Harvard, Alain Locke was the first African American Rhodes Scholar. He studied in Oxford, England in the early 1900s and went on to become an important voice during the Harlem Renaissance through his writings and his teaching career at Howard University.

Education, careers, achievement, and goals, a strong sense of heritage and pride, U is for Universities and the opportunities that they provide.

Since the United States was first founded, African Americans fought hard for the right to vote, even though government leaders often tried to take this right away.

After the Civil War, new laws made it impossible for African Americans to vote. The Grandfather Clause only let people vote whose grandfather had voted. Since most African Americans in the South had been enslaved, their grandfathers couldn't vote, so neither could they. A poll tax was often charged which also made it too expensive to vote.

In 1964 black and white student volunteers flocked to Mississippi during Freedom Summer. These volunteers registered African Americans to vote. They set up Freedom Schools to teach about voting and political rights.

The Voting Rights Act of 1965 got rid of poll taxes and other racial restrictions on voting. For the first time in history, many African Americans were now able to vote.

Cast your ballot in the box.
Let your voice be heard.
V is for the right to Vote
and make a difference in this world.

Since colonial days, important milestones in literature have been achieved. In 1773, Phillis Wheatley became the first African American to publish a book of poems. In the late 1700s, Benjamin Banneker was well known for his series of almanacs. William Cooper Nell published a history book in 1855 about the participation of black patriots in the Revolutionary War. In the late 1800s, William Wells Brown and Harriet E. Wilson each published the first novels written by African Americans.

Many writers, including Gwendolyn Brooks, Alex Haley, Toni Morrison, and Alice Walker, have received outstanding awards and honors such as the Pulitzer Prize or the Nobel Prize for literature.

Maya Angelou read her poem "On the Pulse of Morning" in 1993 at the inauguration of President Bill Clinton.

In 1993 Rita Dove became the first African American to serve as poet laureate of the United States.

O, The Oprah Magazine is published by TV talk show host, Oprah Winfrey, who also interviews numerous writers for her book club. With her heartwarming style, Oprah inspires her listeners and readers to reach for the stars.

Storytellers, historians, and poets
writing words that are wonderful and wise.
W is for Writers
and the winners of the Pulitzer Prize.

Not everyone believed in Dr. Martin Luther King Jr.'s methods of nonviolent protest during the Civil Rights Movement. Malcolm X, an outspoken leader of the Nation of Islam, drew large crowds who supported a more militant stand.

At first, mostly as a result of racial violence aimed against his family when he was young, Malcolm X argued that blacks and whites could not live successfully together. As the Civil Rights Movement progressed, however, he eventually changed his views and started to believe all people should learn to live together as equals. His life was tragically cut short when he was assassinated in 1965.

Today, Malcolm X has become a symbol of heritage, power, pride, and self-determination. Through his legacy, he continues to motivate and inspire people to continue the fight for human rights.

A voice in the struggle for equality,
X   a symbol of power and might,
is for Malcolm X,
an activist for civil rights.

Y is for York, a mountain man with the Lewis and Clark expedition. His brave explorations opened the way to new worlds for the next generation.

Yy

Skillful frontiersman, York helped make the Lewis and Clark expedition a success. He was one of many African American explorers whose courage and love for adventure paved the way for future generations.

Archeologists found giant stone heads in Mexico where a group of people called the Olmecs lived around 800 B.C.E. These statues have huge faces that look like people from Africa. This leads scholars to believe that African explorers reached the Americas many years before Columbus.

During colonial days, Africans arrived in the Americas as conquistadors, sailors, explorers, and slaves. Juan Garrido fought with Cortez to conquer Mexico City. Nuflo de Olano was with Balboa's expedition when they first sighted the Pacific Ocean. Estevanico led an exploring party through the southwestern United States. In 1565 men skilled as blacksmiths, soldiers, and farmers helped establish the settlement of St. Augustine in what is now known as Florida.

After James Beckwourth discovered what is now called Beckwourth Pass, wagon trains could travel to California safely through the Sierra Nevada Mountains.

In 1909 arctic explorer Matthew Henson became co-discoverer of the North Pole.

Astronauts such as "Guy" Bluford, Ronald McNair, Mae Jemison, and Michael Anderson are trained to explore outer space, the new frontier.

In the years leading up to the Civil War, many African American churches became stops along the Underground Railroad. Fugitive slaves were sheltered in secret hiding places on their way north to Canada, which was often referred to as the Promised Land.

During the struggle to abolish slavery, throughout the Civil Rights Movement, and continuing today, the church has been a center of faith, strength, and hope for count-less African Americans. More than just a religious gathering place, the church has also been the stage for political meetings and community events.

In 1794 Richard Allen founded Bethel Church in Philadelphia. It became the mother church of the African Methodist Episcopal (A.M.E.) Church, with Allen elected as its first bishop. From the pulpit of Bethel Church, Richard Allen and other abolitionist leaders led the fight against the American Colonization Society, which tried to forcibly relocate free blacks to Liberia, Africa before the Civil War.

Peter Williams Sr. was instrumental in founding the African Methodist Episcopal Zion (A.M.E.Z.) Church in New York City in the late 1700s.

Jarena Lee was the first woman preacher in the A.M.E. Church. Because of her dedi-cated service and commitment, she paved the way for other women evangelists to spread their faith.

Congregations gathering to sing a hymn,
church members joining hand in hand,
Z is for Zion and churches of faith
along the journey to the Promised Land.

Zz

Selected Reference List

Altman, Susan. 1997. *The Encyclopedia of African-American Heritage*. New York: Facts On File, Inc.

Appiah, Kwame Anthony & Gates, Henry Louis, Jr. 1999. *Africana: The Encyclopedia of the African and African American Experience*. New York: Basic Civitas Books.

Bennett, Lerone, Jr. 1988. *Before the Mayflower*. New York: Penguin Books.

The Bicycle & the West. http://cliffhanger76.tripod.com/bikewest/1897/ (Accessed April 1, 2005).

Breaking New Ground: African American Senators. http://www.senate.gov/pagelayout/history/h_multi_sections_and_teasers/Photo_Exhibit_African_American_Senators.htm (Accessed November 27, 2006).

Bush Picks Rice to Succeed Powell. http://www.cnn.com/2004/ALLPOLITICS/11/16/rice.powell/ (Accessed August 5, 2005).

Collins, Charles M. & Cohen, David. 1993. *The African Americans: A Celebration of Achievement*. New York: Viking Studio Books.

Crew, Spencer R. 1987. *Field to Factory: Afro-American Migration 1915-1940*. Washington, D.C.: Smithsonian Institution.

Editors of Time-Life Books. 1993. *African Americans: Voices of Triumph: Perseverance, Leadership, and Creative Fire*. Richmond, Virginia: Time-Life Books.

Faith Ringgold – Biography. http://www.faithringgold.com (Accessed August 3, 2005).

The First Black Americans. http://www.usnews.com/usnews/news/articles/070121/29african.htm (Accessed February 21, 2007).

Follow the Drinking Gourd. http://www.nsa.gov/publications/publi00011.cfm (Accessed May 24, 2005).

Fort Mose: Free African Settlement. http://www.oldcity.com/sites/mose/(Accessed March 3, 2005).

From Indentured Servitude to Racial Slavery. http://www.pbs.org/wgbh/aia/part1/1narr3.html (Accessed November 1, 2004).

Gates, Henry Louis, Jr. & West, Cornel. 2000. *The African American Century*. New York: The Free Press.

Green, Richard L., ed. 1993. *African Kings and Queens*. Chicago: Empak Publishing Company.

Green, Richard L., ed. 1996. *A Salute to Black Civil Rights Leaders*. Chicago: Empak Publishing Company.

Green, Richard L., ed. 1996. *A Salute to Blacks in the Federal Government*. Chicago: Empak Publishing Company.

Harley, Sharon. 1995. *The Timetables of African-American History*. New York: Simon & Schuster.

Harriet Powers. http://xroads.virginia.edu/~UG97/quilt/harriet.html (Accessed July 28, 2005).

Harriet Powers: A Freed Slave Tells Stories Through Quilting. http://www.historyofquilts.com/hpowers.html (Accessed July 28, 2005).

Haskins, Jim. 1992. *Against All Opposition*. New York: Walker and Company.

Hine, Darlene Clark, ed. 1993. *Black Women in America*. New York: Carlson Publishing Inc.

Hornsby, Alton, Jr. 1991. *Chronology of African-American History*. Detroit: Gale Research Inc.

Kaplan, Sidney and Kaplan, Emma Nogrady. 1989. *The Black Presence in the Era of the American Revolution*. Amherst: The University of Massachusetts Press.

Katz, William Loren. 1995. *Eyewitness: A Living Documentary of the African American Contribution to American History*. New York: Simon & Schuster.

Marooned: Africans in the Americas 1500-1750. http://www.jayikislakfoundation.org/millennium-exhibit/burnside1.htm (Accessed March 3, 2005).

Maya Angelou. http://www.mayaangelou.com (Accessed August 9, 2005).

McKissack, Patricia & McKissack, Fredrick. 1994. *The Royal Kingdoms of Ghana, Mali, and Songhay*. New York: Henry Holt.

Michael P. Anderson. http://space.about.com/cs.columbialosses/a/anderson.htm (Accessed August 10, 2005).

Miles, Johnnie H. et al. 2001. *Almanac of African American Heritage*. Paramus, New Jersey: Prentice Hall Press.

Mystery of Va.'s First Slaves Is Unlocked 400 Years Later. http://www.washingtonpost.com/wp-dyn/content/article/2006/09/02/AR2006090201097_pf.html (Accessed February 21, 2007).

NASA – Space Shuttle Columbia and Her Crew. http://www.nasa.gov/Columbia/crew/profile_michaela.html (Accessed August 10, 2005).

Nash, Gary B. 1974. *Red, White, and Black*. Englewood Cliffs, New Jersey: Prentice-Hall, Inc. Padgett, Debby (Media Relations Manager, Jamestown-Yorktown Foundation), in discussion with the author, November 2004.

Patrick, Diane. 1998. *Amazing African American History: A Book of Answers for Kids*. New York: John Wiley & Sons, Inc.

Ploski, Harry A. & Williams, James. 1989. *The Negro Almanac*. New York: Gale Research Inc.

The Rita Dove HomePage. http://www.people.virginia.edu/~rfd4b (Accessed August 9, 2005).

Salzman, Jack. 1993. *The African-American Experience: Macmillan Information Now Encyclopedia*. New York: Macmillan Library Reference USA.

Sanders, Nancy I. 2000. *A Kid's Guide to African American History*. Chicago: Chicago Review Press.

Sertima, Ivan Van. 1976. *They Came Before Columbus*. New York: Random House.

Smith, Jessie Carney. 1994. *Black Firsts*. Detroit: Visible Ink Press.

Stewart, Jeffrey C. 1996. *1001 Things Everyone Should Know About African American History*. New York: Main Street Books.

Tuskegee Airmen to Be Honored in Washington. http://abcnews.go.com/GMA/story?id=2991630.

Vonetta Flowers. http://www.vonettaflowers.com/ (Accessed July 23, 2005).

Williams, Michael W., Editor. 1993. *The African American Encyclopedia*. New York: Marshall Cavendish.

Wynton Marsalis. http://www.wyntonmarsalis.com (Accessed August 16, 2005).